O Garden-Dweller

poems by

Laura Reece Hogan

Finishing Line Press
Georgetown, Kentucky

O Garden-Dweller

Copyright © 2017 by Laura Reece Hogan
ISBN 978-1-63534-271-0 First Edition
All rights reserved under International and Pan-American Copyright Conventions.
No part of this book may be reproduced in any manner whatsoever without written permission from the publisher, except in the case of brief quotations embodied in critical articles and reviews.

ACKNOWLEDGMENTS

My thanks to the editors of the following publications in which some of the poems selected for this chapbook previously appeared:

Faith Hope and Fiction, "Sunrise after the Storm" and "Angel of Dark and Fire" (January 16, 2016)
The Christian Century, "Organic Ink" (April 27, 2016)
PILGRIM: A Journal of Catholic Experience, "Behold You Were Within Me" (May 15, 2016)
The Penwood Review, "Pantoum of the Tinderbox" (volume 20, number 1, Spring 2016)
Plum Tree Tavern, "Rain Comes in the Fourth Year" (September 4, 2016)
The Windhover, "Nocturne" (volume 21.1, Spring 2017)

Publisher: Leah Maines

Editor: Christen Kincaid

Cover Art: Kathy Steckel, www.kathysteckel.com

Author Photo: Debbie Walton of Walton Portrait Gallery

Cover Design: Elizabeth Maines McCleavy

Printed in the USA on acid-free paper.
Order online: www.finishinglinepress.com
also available on amazon.com

Author inquiries and mail orders:
Finishing Line Press
P. O. Box 1626
Georgetown, Kentucky 40324
U. S. A.

Table of Contents

Behold You Were Within Me 1

The Edge of Who 2

Torchlight 4

Nocturne 5

Catch Us the Foxes 6

On Adoring You 7

Song of the Sown 8

His Emblem over Me 9

Pantoum of the Tinderbox 10

Angel of Dark and Fire 12

Earth on Fire 14

Evidence of a Burning Bush 16

Rain Comes in the Fourth Year 17

Winter Shoots 18

Sunrise after the Storm 19

Sacrament of Spring 20

The Language of Open 21

The Joy Tree 22

Some Bird Soaring 24

Organic Ink 26

For him whom my heart loves.
Song of Songs 3:2

"O garden-dweller,
>my friends are listening for your voice,
>let me hear it!"
>Song of Songs 8:13

The Song of Songs, found in Hebrew and Christian scriptures, conveys in poetic form the intimate love between the bride and the groom, interpreted often in tradition as the human soul and the divine. The Song captures the spiritual journey of the soul toward its God through expression of the delight which the soul and the Beloved find in one another and their garden, the soul's despair in the absence of the Beloved and the consequent experience of loss and pain, and finally the union of the soul and Beloved.

This collection of poetry is inspired by a garden and its residents, a historic drought, a wildfire and its aftermath, experience of the divine in the everyday, and the Song of Songs. Several of the poems echo moments found in the Song and other scripture, and the poems are generally arranged according to the arc of the Song.

I am grateful to Leah Maines and Christen Kincaid of Finishing Line Press for their kind editorial assistance. Emphatic thanks to my dear friend and poeming partner, Elizabeth Kuelbs, and to my loving family, Mike, Caitlin, Connor, and Amanda.

Behold You Were Within Me

How you love the humble hiding place
The fuzzy green purpled promise of apricot,
The blade of grass quaking with
    the still small voice of breeze unheard.

There—in glorious sheen of upright palms
I glimpse you. The swaying frond, her glancing sparkle,
and the steady love of sunshine—a moment's trio
    in one humming, joyful dance.

You favor damp folds of faded foxgloves.
Bide with barren branches aching for rebirth.
Secret yourself among silent seeds with power
    to fall and die yet live and rise.

Impossible—yet in earthy human jars
You dwell, wrapped in rustic sinew
Treasure buried in dust—or stardust?
    Waiting for the fumbling heart to startle,
        to leap!
            To find.

The Edge of Who

You stand on the edge
    of the who you have yet to be
Sunbeams do not pick and choose
but gladly crown mock orange and orange alike
    with jeweled glow of springtime honesty.
Their cleaving sun-embered embrace
illuminates, fires, transforms
orange blossom into the tangy exhale of heaven—
Inhale, my goodness, stop and inhale goodness;
    Breathe the
    Breath
    Be
    and behold an achingly blazing beauty only for you, beloved.

Yet we with muted eye grapple
        for the demarcation
Perhaps dazzled, perhaps forgetting
    that the now is filled to the full with God.
Brilliance plays on, in
        along,
            beside,
                below
    the edges of your who,
        who while looking
            for
                the
                      breadcrumb path
    overlooked the crystalline lantern
    of his who of you, inside.

He shimmers and sparks and speaks
    silent firecrackers of love
Pulls at your heart (no, there is no mistake)
Meets your eyes with deep (a kiss by another name)
Draws you with peace (yes, and resounding joy):

>   Be with me
>   and begin to Be, beloved,
>
> I am the possible impossible and
>   the unexpected delight
> Edges, even yours, curl and vanish
>   in love's transfiguring light.

Torchlight

Divine torches line
the way home.
Sugar maple
ruby fires
burn with delight.

Do they hide
inner suns?
They ignite
the very air
with scarlet glow.

In rushing joy
blazing hands stir,
caress coiling wind;
the dancing image
of living light.

In their ardor they
let go.
Crimson jewels fly,
become carpet,
vanish.

Naked branches yawn,
drowse in the gale,
dream of the hand that
kindles, stokes fire,
brings to life again.

Nocturne

Silk of a thousand shades flows from your throat, night notes billow, float, dance in the sleeping garden, tangle of rosebush the shadowed lectern of your liturgy. Star beams cannot find your gray body but fiery sparks issue

from open beak: scrub jay shriek melts into lilt of robin, goldfinch warble sharpens to hawk cry, hoot owl, medley of sky and tree. You wing wide, embrace all nations of the tongue, a writer of icons, singing doorways of egg and gold

and open eyes, a call to the soaring beyond. You chant the quilt of creation, hymn to fingers that wove the fabric of melody, conducted patterns of feather, flight and fugue. Now the phoebe's sweet chirp, swallow's chatter, scraping

crow-caw, you swallow the wide world whole just to croon your divine office, embroider blessing on the hours, lauds in blackness. Mockingbird, you settle on my chimney top like a church steeple, trilling frogsong, the cricket's hum,

burbling laugh of the neighbor child. You chat, you rasp, chirrup, scold. You sing sunlight in the darkness, telling cocoons and keening coyotes how we were knitted to love, endure, and even in the cleft of night, joy in spilling praise.

Catch Us the Foxes

In the silvery shadow of
All Hallows Eve
you appeared, blue fox.

(Catch us the foxes, beloved.
Their teeth cut sharp on the vines.)

You crush moonflowers,
spoil with careless mouth.
You prefer the struggle of
a sparrow to her flight.

(Their teeth cut sharp on the vines.)

Nimble feet so quick to
run away forever without
the wink of a farewell.

(Catch us the foxes, the little foxes
that damage the vineyards.)

Your proud shrub of a tail—
trailing, yet governing.
You never knew yourself.

(They damage the vineyards, and
our vineyards are in bloom!)

Less blue fox than ghost,
you stared frozen in my light,
abandoned your place, a vapor
vanishing into the chill dark,
a specter among specters.

And our vineyards bloom sweet
in the sun.

On Adoring You

In dark cords of night you weave for me
a cocoon of yourself. Splinters for silk,
thorns your thread, a love poured, an emptied
truth. I drink, in stripped unknowing. I long
to emerge winged, a bloom from black earth,
for love is stronger than death.

At sunrise you plait a pink-embered sky
with chattering towhees. Dew shines, a
needlework of mercy. Sugar maples
reach skyward, bud purple. You stitch
starlings, silvered chaparral, morning
glories, the faces I kiss—I feast on
the oranges of your love.

In strands mysterious I delight in you
in yet a third way. In the cellar under
silenced words, you wait, your impossible
wine in stone water jars. Golden threads
embrace, embroider, draw me,
astonished, to you.

Song of the Sown

Who is the seedling heartbeat of the tree?
You were, and are, and ever shall be;
Yet, she-who-is-not also might come to be—
In muddy, graced intertwine of root and leaf.

Deep within, she winds and waits,
Close in the kernel's embrace;
Deep without, horizonless yield,
Sheaves, glinting crown of run race.

Yet between; ah, the joyful, painful between
Of simply with—a disintegrating unity
As sown seed gives over self to sod—*Selah*
And becomes green unfolding we.

His Emblem over Me
    For Saint Teresa of Calcutta

Nowhere to lay your head,
nothing to call your own.
Why must it cost so much
to empty and to roam?

Holed up inside my heart
the stubborn will clings;
you turn out the precious pocket,
you bruise and break the seams.

Now, beloved, come to me,
I am wounded, dark, and blue—
your colors unfurl over me,
I suffer in search of you.

I wait in roiling silence,
but no hand is at the lock.
Only absence, empty holes,
and smashing on the rock.

Am I not your cherished bride?
Yet I am abandoned, lost.
Your neglect I hide; I smile, I
wear the poverty of your cross.

Nowhere to lay my head
makes me yet your own;
nothing save imprint of you
on yielded heart, our home.

Pantoum of the Tinderbox

Even now you could send a drop
For the beating box of my brittle heart
Years now so dry, no rain, no refrain
Your lush green melody hushed away

From the beating box of my brittle heart
You hide in shifting scorched sand
Lush green melody a hushed memory
I wander this, your parched desert

You hide in searing scorched sand
My charred lips crack, peel in pain
I wander this, your parched desert
My throat rattles stripped prayer

My charred lips crack, appeal in vain
Fingers twist like dying vines
My throat rattles, stripped of prayer
Once verdant land crumbles to stubble

Fingers twist like dying vines
You say only, "I want it dry"
My verdant land crumbles to stubble
Again: "I am building a fire in you."

You say only, "I want it dry"
So dry all my bones ache and cry
Again: "I am building a fire in you."
Drought presses on within, without

So dry all my bones ache to cry:
Strike up the lightning march, then!
Drought presses on within, without
St. John tells me you are living fire

Strike the lightning match, then!
Your gasping, arid box awaits
St. John tells me you are loving fire
Turn tinder to bright ardent flame

Your gasping, arid box awaits
Years now so dry, no rain, no refrain
Turn tender, ignite ardent flame
Even now you could drop the match.

Angel of Dark and Fire

My angel most certainly
dwells in darkness and fire.
She my assigned warrior
battles night and chaos.

She lives in the crags
between asleep and awake.
Sword glinting, eyes a
steely might in my favor.

Born fire from Fire
she is of the Fire I love.
You, set in my heart,
set as a seal, burning.

You encircle me, you
make flame her buckler.
Why should I fear?
She prevails, powerful
sentry in this world; yet
she dissolves, forceful
magnet to the next.

Darkness is yet light
in that kingdom.
A temporary blindness
which opens wide.

My angel stands in
divine darkness,
the black hole of
her unseen weight
compels, urges me
into lightness, a
surrender to brightness.

In her there is no fear.
I long for such wings.
Reaching sightless
my embrace meets
the alchemy of
your Fire. Cares forgotten,
I take flight.

Earth on Fire

A haze of smoke hangs high, a red-eyed
canopy of uncertain danger, strange, yet more
and more familiar with each passing news cycle,
as day follows brittle day. Drought has pressed

grass into crunchy brown scrub, plum trees into
tinder, heartbeats of the phoebe into a clattering for
water, seed, relief. Yet what comes is fire, relentless
inferno, licking red tongues of destruction, flames

clasping hands with scorching sirocco winds,
outstripping jack rabbits, incinerating chaparral,
walnuts, oaks, all one in the blazing terror of wild,
consuming hunger. The wisdom of birds grows silent.

(Yet, did not you say you came to set the earth on fire?)

Now listen to what was left behind. The very soil lies
coal black, hills turned to ash, to nothing; every contour
bared in mourning, broken only by harsh bony fingers of
ebony oak corpse, stabbing through the side of moonscape.

(Yet, did not you say you wished it were already blazing?)

Let me tell you what I see there, on the shoulders of
the charred foothills. What was fire, and death, and the
end, has become a new Jerusalem. She is shadowed
yet beautiful. She says, "Do not stare at me because

I am dark, because living fire has burned me." What flames have turned ash, the beloved embraces. What lies barren births anew, a shared, open heart, suffering yet transformed, transforming, still in bride-clothes.

A seed lies there, one that only knows to break open at the caress of its natural mother, fire.

Though we sit in embers, the dead grain lives, pushes root, splits hard dirt, and hard kin. Our earth blazing (yes, already blazing), we hold fast, entrust our acorns to bags that do not wear out, nor fear the flame.

Evidence of a Burning Bush

Bed of blackened sugarbush bones lie,
a truth, now scorched claw struck down,

up in flames, obscure monument, a history,
a future. A burned bush, charred fallen hand,

a fist of silence, burning once for all and
none watched. Not burning bush untouched,

caressed by God in flame yet unconsumed,
ablaze on Horeb. These ebony fingers pointless,

purposefully indicate heavenward, soundless
shout, "I am evidence" and " I am beginning,"

an end accomplished, a sign for all to see, the
blind will not. Which, I wonder, is the stronger

weaker case for the groping heart in anguished
hope, the bush which burns bright without hurt

searing evermore, or the sugarbush that knows
unknown agony of inferno, brokenness, a death,

a life unsuspected in divine rejoinder, firedeath
birthing firelife, ashes for seed burst into being?

Rain Comes in the Fourth Year

Drought-flamed leaves wake
in bewilderment under
the unfamiliar caress of
liquid mercy,
a strange drenching of hope.

Sugar maple fingers drip
myrrh, precious dew
persimmons gather courage,
gasping pepper trees and
wasting cottontails revive.

Roots remember
Elijah casting prayer
over the sea long ago;
changed hearts
watered the dust of Carmel.

Every living thing
drinks, colors deepen,
darken with wet blessing.
The collective breath draws damp,
sighs relief.

At last you have turned your face
to us, wreathed in cloud.
Your gentle rain
quiet as the prayer
of our very cells.

And the towhees and larks,
darting acrobats
in air washed
clean
of the dry multitude of regrets,
pierce the sky with
reaching cascades of joy.

Winter Shoots

In hailstorm of sightless swirl, the chaos close,
closer, you separate the light from the dark, you
reveal a part of you, a spark in me, a tender green

pod of peace, pearl of great price, here within, quiet.
Peace or pea or pearl, clasped in cloistered hiding,
cloaked yet shining. She speaks courage to me: look

to my new swelling verdant belly, not the dark lands.
Those decay, they fall away, but this remains, this anchor
of future, not past. You lament calendar and clock, you

open gates to flood, you usher away hope like an empty-
eyed mourner. But see here—lush tranquility! Promise
endures here, tucked secure, sowed. It will not disappoint.

Even beneath your notice (notice how you do not notice),
the upsurging growth, the bursting fruit, perfect out of
imperfect, fertile out of futile, mysterious globe of seed

stirs awake, a hardborn faith, planted all along, sprouting
in the season of hollowed heartbeat—vision of victory,
gazing straight at night, breathing sweet, budding, climbing.

Sunrise after the Storm

Dark sky shatters, in shards at last
Your sudden brilliance pierces,
Scatters blackness and broken thought,
Sets the spectral horizon ablaze.

Your luminous kisses brush
Leaden bruised cheeks, so hurt
Touching, lighting afire—
Sparking slivers of blue promise.

You have come for me after all
And given me this,
In airy paper and nimbus ribbon—
Unmistakable hope.

Sacrament of Spring

Heavy with hibernation and eye-blink, I
flatten dewy baby green blades. I wonder
why my silver-tipped bear hair belongs here

in the glorious garden of fresh bursting pear
blossoms, where even branches birth red tender
shoots, newborn fists opening in innocent

praise. Light and rain and life! they cry, reach
to suckle sunshine. My hip scoffs, grumbles
an unwelcome antiphon. But you too, whisper

a thousand verdant buds on rejoicing hills
—you too! Fragrant roses draw, tumble me
on knees in invitation to inhale incense,

cinnamon crescendo, cardamom of angels.
Goldfinches swell the song—You too too too.
You new new new. Sight and sound and

scent of the sacrament of spring surge into
my heart, a living lighting strike of joy, kiss
electric, sparking blooms unknown to begin.

The Language of Open

At the very center, pistil to petal
you remain in my rose, all fragrance.
You are honey and lemons in my tea.
I know your knock on my whittled-down
hut of abandonment, abode of withered hope,
the disappointed country, cut hard to stubble.

The language of open is not spoken here, but
one of a bitter kind, biting, not abiding.
You know your knock on the black uneven
timber of my last door, the one I cannot see,
the one built by those neglectful architects
the grasshoppers, when I wanted, oh, I wanted
                                        the butterflies.

I know your knock, you know my wooden knot
the hurt resistance, a sullen swelling silence.
You subdue, you submerge with your peace,
honeyed fingers and citrus smile, balm of Gilead.

So much adoring poured out, overflowing my
teacup, my acorn of anguish, the very universe
brought to bear, to touch, to hold, to cure my cold,
to coax apart, to warm, delight, to cross over a
forbidding threshold with rush of winged light.
                              Unweighted, I forget.

Honeybee gold in the glow of coming free,
my petals reach wide, soak sunshine
unfurl the incense of an answer, open
the drawbridge, spilling out one short
syllable of surprised dawnbreak,
surrendering the lot, joying in loss,
flaming into the splendid bloom of yes.

The Joy Tree

Her dragon scales startle, a bark of cutting thorn.
As a tender sapling, sharp green exclamation points
warned the world of her self-containment. Now
time-thick and wise, her silver spikes declare:
She has other food of which you know not.

Silk-Floss stretches, reaches high, traces flight of
falcons. She aches to soar, burst bloom but knows
the irony of her name; bristles rip silk, barbs belie
angels. Needles prick, but the finches do not mind.

In spring, woody whorls of hope ring round inside.
She ponders the parade of daffodils, irises, azaleas.
Lilies unveil, daisies lift sunny heads. Boxwoods
bud, swallowtails sail through her fingers.

Summer boasts asters, roses, marigolds, blue sugar
berries. Jacarandas pop purple, birds of paradise
sing her to sleep on wafting spice. Peaches glow
like young dashing suns, globes of juicy promise.

Still she waits. Her thorns reveal her difficulty, a
passion out of season, empty. No warm budding
petals for her, no opening peals of mirth. Yet beneath
the spines her sap runs sure, sweet, ticks out her time.
She knows her creator knows his creation.

Autumn chills her roots. Persimmons catch gold fire.
Others flutter candy apple, butter, ginger. No show
of scarlet silk for her. She grimaces, groans, drops
her drab downcast leaves. It is finished.
And who would have thought any more of her?

Winter breaks, she wakes bright, shocks the sparrows.
Scrub jays scream, squirrels stare. In the gloom she
blushes pink blossoms, stands unfolded, complete.
Her limbs dazzle, robed in radiance. In the darkness
of the barren month, undisturbed in patient longing,
she reaches full flower of love—joy.

Some Bird Soaring

Things are falling away
steadily under
the chisel
of Michelangelo's creator.

Slabs of alabaster self
pain, crash, pile.
Who knew I did not need
such cold weight?

Bittersweet
but finely balanced.

Pared away
but smooth and light.

Inscribed
yet gliding free.

A sharper silhouette.

Translucent wings
flex, honed hawk
thin to let the sun
shine through.

A traveler squints
against the glare,
seeking direction,
a chart for change.
There:

some bird, soaring!

Her face glows.

I leave it to her
to puzzle out
the markings.

I just fly.

Organic Ink

Petals unfold from your tongue, you speak crimson
velvet freshness into being. An opening bud of careful
precision, a floral life floating on your breath, bees, and boundary.

You expand a mystery of molecules, at your word atomic spice
springs into breeze; you dizzy hummingbirds, intoxicate butterflies.
Shining beams play, shimmer, light your Shulamite, invite a tango.

You draw. Come, find my notes poured out in the garden, etched among
lemons and limes. See, the lost apricot awakens! Sweet shoots adorn
black crumbling branches. On every cell I inscribe: what was dead is alive.

You wait for me to discover your love among the leaves and thorns,
(will I perceive it?) your hidden blossom of wonder, a shy heart-shaped
valentine of third heaven, a sachet for this moment, a marked downbeat

of song, a bodily inhale of my eyes and skin and hair and breath. Filled
with rising melody, your unspoken lyrics whispered on wind, I join
your written roses in swaying dance, in blood-red bloom of belonging.

Laura Reece Hogan's poetry has appeared in *The Christian Century, Faith Hope and Fiction, PILGRIM: A Journal of Catholic Experience, The Penwood Review, Plum Tree Tavern,* and *The Windhover.* She is the author of *I Live, No Longer I: Paul's Spirituality of Suffering, Transformation, and Joy* (Wipf & Stock, 2017), which examines the spirituality of the apostle Paul. Her essay, "The Brightness of Bones," was featured in *Spirituality.*

Laura earned a B.A. from Rice University in Houston, Texas, a J.D. from the University of California, Los Angeles School of Law, and a M.A. in theology from St. John's Seminary in Camarillo, California. Laura is a professed Third Order Carmelite. She lives with her family in Southern California.

www.ingramcontent.com/pod-product-compliance
Lightning Source LLC
LaVergne TN
LVHW041513070426
835507LV00012B/1527